MW00944007

Moments

of

Divine Intimacy

Devotions for Thirty-one Days

Chaplain Harold L. Christmann
Commander, Chc, USNR, Retired

ISBN 978-1-64140-398-6 (paperback)
ISBN 978-1-64140-399-3 (digital)

Christian Faith Publishing, Inc.
832 Park Avenue
Meadville, PA 16335
www.christianfaithpublishing.com

Printed in the United States of America

About the Author

Ch. Christmann was ordained as a minister in the Christian Church (Disciples of Christ). Under this endorsement, he pastored First Christian Church, El Cajon, California, and Frayser Christian Church, Memphis, Tennessee. He also served on active duty as a navy chaplain. Additionally, he served as a clinical jail chaplain, VA hospital chaplain, and a hospice chaplain.

Ch. Christmann also had ministerial credentials with the Assembly of God denomination. He was assistant professor of religion at Evangel College, which is now Evangel University. While on leave from the college, he served as a navy chaplain in Vietnam. Ch. Christmann also served as a clinical chaplain for a maximum security prison in Boise, Idaho.

Ch. Christmann currently has ministerial credentials with the Christian Church (Disciples of Christ) northwest region. He has retired as a navy reserve chaplain with the rank of commander.

He has a BA from Drury University in Springfield, Missouri; a Masters of Divinity degree from Christian Theological Seminary, in Indianapolis, Indiana; and a Masters in Public Administration degree from Boise State University in Boise, Idaho.

Moreover, Ch. Christmann has completed fifteen quarters clinical training certified by the Association of Clinical Pastoral Education. His first quarter was completed at the Medical Center for Federal Prisoners in Springfield, Missouri. Ch. Christmann competed a 12-month internship at the Hillcrest Medical Center in Tulsa, Oklahoma.

Ch. Christmann and Janet, his wife of forty years, now reside in a retirement center, Ventura Townehouse, Ventura, California.

Contents

Foreword

But I say, walk by the Spirit and you will not
gratify the desires of the flesh. (Galatians 5:16)

If we live by the Spirit, let us also walk
by the Spirit. (Galatians 5:25)

In these verses, the apostle Paul admonishes us to
walk or live by the Holy Spirit.

Living daily in the empowerment of and in step
with the Holy Spirit can be somewhat elusive for
many Christ-followers. For some, it may feel like
chasing after the wind. So much of what has been
written about the gifts and ministry of the Holy Spirit
focuses on Holy Spirit empowerment and equip-
ping for ministry inside the four walls of the church
buildings.

The Holy Spirit has come to give life to every
Christ-follower, to empower every Christ-follower
to share their faith, to live in victory, to love more

fully, to pray with greater intimacy, and to experience ongoing illumination and application of the word of God. It is the Holy Spirit who daily enriches our lives with the fruit and gifts of the Holy Spirit.

Ch. Christmann's devotional, Moments of Divine Intimacy, offers daily readings that give insight on the life of the Holy Spirit that are beneficial for each and every Christ-follower. Ch. Christmann weaves his experiences with the Holy Spirit into his devotional, offering the reader a window into the ministry of the Paraclete or the One called alongside. The Holy Spirit is the one Jesus has given us to come alongside of us to do life with us. The reader will find inspirational insight into the ministry of the Spirit for their own daily lives as they reflect on their devotion. They will find practical understanding and application from the scriptures regarding living daily with the Holy Spirit in each day of devotional reading.

This little devotional offers a good launching place for growing and deepening our daily relationship with the Holy Spirit. You will find yourself challenged to look inside yourself. It will challenge and encourage you to walk hand in hand with the Holy

Spirit on a daily basis as you learn to recognize his presence each and every day.

Rev. Ted Pugh, MA
Pastor, Ventura First Assembly of God
Ventura, CA, July 1, 2017

Introduction

For over sixty years, I have been serving the Lord. He has given me diverse and exciting paths of ministry. These paths have included serving as a pastor, as a navy chaplain, and as a professor of religion at a Christian college (now a university) and also as a clinical correctional and hospital chaplain and a certified pastoral counselor.

It has not always been a smooth path, not because of him, but because of my own stubbornness and willfulness. But through it all, God's grace has been sufficient.

Through all of this, the Lord has taught me some practical principles and given me some personal experiences that have helped me cope with my circumstances in a redemptive way. I want to share some of these with the prayer that others may be helped to deepen their walk with the Lord and experience their moments of divine intimacy.

I am indebted to John Bevere, a well-known evangelist, who made me realize how much God wanted to have intimacy with us. In one of his teaching tapes, he stated that everything God has done in Christ is for the purpose of having intimacy with us.

I thought, *Wow! Christ didn't just die for our sins or for our salvation. He died to remove all barriers to intimacy with God. Wow!*

A quick survey of the Bible supports this. In the garden, in the cool of the evening, God was with Adam. Abraham responded to God's intimate call. Moses and the burning bush, Elijah and the whirlwind, Isaiah in the temple to worship, David dancing before the Lord, and many others—they all were experiencing moments of intimacy with the Lord. We can trace this through the New Testament—Jesus and his disciples, Jesus post-resurrection appearances, and ultimately the coming of the Holy Spirit to give us permanent intimacy. How gracious and generous is our God and his Son.

So as I reviewed my walk with the Lord, I realized that all through it, he has given me many moments of divine intimacy. These have come through inspired insights through his word and supernatural manifestation of the Holy Spirit.

This will not be a theological analysis but based on personal experiences. These are not the result of being spiritually elite. It is simply the work of a loving God through his Holy Spirit, which is available to all believers.

In the 1960s, there was a widespread move of the Holy Spirit throughout all denominations; Christians, Catholics, and all groups of Protestants were receiving what was called the baptism with the Holy Spirit similar to the day of Pentecost in Acts 2.

I resisted this at first, but then became convinced it was biblical and received it.

The direction of my ministry was changed. Some of this is described in this book.

I respect those who may not accept this experience. I intend no offense. I am just sharing my experience of intimacy. I urge all believers to seek their own moments of intimacy.

I have sought to give credit for ideas or thoughts of others who have influenced me.

Yet, I realize that I have probably absorbed thoughts and ideas over the years that may seem like mine. If so, I ask for your understanding and forgiveness.

As you read this, ask the Lord to speak to you and give you your own moments of intimacy.

I have arranged these writings as a devotional reading for thirty-one days. Each meditation shares an experience or teaching that was personal and helped me to strengthen my relationship with the Lord. May they help you to do the same, I have shared these experiences to encourage Christian's that such moments of intimacy are possible for all believers. For those as yet who don't believe, come to Christ in faith and experience your own intimate moments. This is my prayer for you.

I urge any unbeliever who may read this book to seek out the truth about Jesus Christ, who he is, and who we can be through faith in him.

The Priority of Grace

For by grace you have been saved through
faith; and this is not your own doing, it is
the gift of God not because of works lest
any man should boast. (Ephesians 2:8)

The starting place for our Christian walk is God's grace. I am mindful of God's grace because I was called to the ministry before I was a Christian. I became a Christian in order to answer God's call on my life. This is God's grace.

So you would assume that this truth would be foundational. However, having not grown up in a church or a religious family, I never heard of God's grace. So as a young seminary student, I became concerned if I was doing enough.

Was I good enough? Was I witnessing enough? Was I winning people to Christ enough?

I heard a preacher on the radio who said that if we were not winning people to Christ daily, we were not good Christians. At least, that is how I heard it. I was pastoring a country church where half of the 600 residents were members of my church. So I really came under self-condemnation. I became concerned that I might not make it to heaven.

I read a book by Watchman Nee on the normal Christian life and discovered that I was saved by grace through faith and not because of works and that my salvation was a gift of God's grace. The load was lifted, and I was free and secure in my salvation.

I wasn't saved by my good works, and I couldn't lose my salvation because of my works. Praise God. This truth has enabled me to weather many spiritual storms and have the assurance that God will never stop loving me or give up on me.

The same is true of you.

Prayer:

Father, I give all of my insecurities, failures, and inadequacies to you.

I choose to walk in confidence and trust that in all circumstances and sin, your grace is sufficient.

Place of Good Works

For we are his workmanship, created in
Christ Jesus for good works, which God
prepared beforehand, that we should
walk in them. (Ephesians 2:10)

So if I am not saved by my good works, what is
the place of good works in the Christian walk? Paul
gives us a clue in Ephesians 2:10. We are not saved
by good works, but if we are a Christian, we will walk
in good works. There is disagreement among sin-
cere Christians on this. But this is my take on this.
When we get married, we are not married because
of good works. We are married because of an act
of commitment to each other in love. Once we have
made this commitment, we are to put that commitment into actions by our loving deeds and care for
each other. One grows out of the other and confirms
the seriousness of our commitment. So we are not

saved by our good works, but our good works are expressions of our commitment.

Consider our present practice of living together before marriage. A couple may show many good deeds of love and care and be responsible in their relationship, but they are not married.

There is no action of commitment. So just as works of love do not make a couple married, good works do not make a person a Christian. Commitment and good works confirm our commitment. We can never earn our salvation by good works. Salvation is a gift. Aren't you glad? We express our love and gratitude by our good works. So serve the Lord with gladness and Love. You have been re-created for good works

So dear Christian, do not be anxious about your good works and salvation. But serve your Lord with gladness and joy because you have been recreated in Christ for this.

Prayer:

Thank you, Lord, that I can serve you with gladness and joy. Thank you, Lord, that I have been given this new life in you not as a burden to earn my salvation but as a life purpose to show how much you love all of us.

How to Increase Faith

So faith comes from what is heard, and
what is heard comes by the preaching
of Christ. (Romans 10:17)

We all have our struggles with faith. I confess that
sometimes, my faith is too small. One reason is
that I allow the visible reality of my circumstances
to intimidate me. What I see and feel seems greater
than the power of God. From the human point of
view what I am asking for seems too much to expect.
Have you noticed that when prayer is asked for such
conditions as cancer there is a gasp of horror. We
are almost overwhelmed by the magnitude of the
condition. Our faith that God can do the impossible
is challenged. The same with other tragedies.

But in the spirit realm, nothing is overwhelming—Jesus feeding the 4000 or restoring sight to
the blind or raising the dead. Jesus did refer to the

faith of his disciples as little faith and to others as great faith. So there is hope for us.

We don't have to stay where we are in faith. We can increase our faith, but not by will power or our own effort.

So how do we do this? Paul gives us the clue in Romans 10. We can increase our faith by hearing the word of Christ. The more we look at what God has promised and embrace that with faith, it will grow. Try it and see.

Prayer:

Lord, help me to look away from what I see and feel to the reality of what you have promised that belongs to us who believe.

Key to Faith

Jesus said to him, "Go your way; our faith has made you well." (Mark10:52)

Jesus told the blind man that his faith had healed him and also that all things were possible for those who believe. These have been challenging statements for me.

They seem to contradict my personal experience. I have not always received what I thought I believed. I have come to realize that I had the wrong idea about faith.

For me, I found myself trying to have faith in my faith. Consequently, I found myself thinking that my faith was not great enough to see the answers. I imagine many of my readers often think that's too much for you to believe or that you don't have enough faith. I discovered that I was trying to have faith in my faith rather than faith in the Lord or his word. Of course, faith in my faith would be inadequate. But faith in him and his word was the key. When we have the proper understanding about faith, all things will be possible. More on this in future meditations.

Prayer:

Lord, you have called us to overcoming faith in you. Forgive us that we have placed our faith in lesser things. Lift our vision to see what faith in you and your word can do.

Nature of Faith

Now faith is the assurance of things hoped for, the conviction of things not seen. (Hebrews 11:1)

So if faith is not in my faith but in the Lord, what is the true nature of faith? The Amplified Bible tells us in this verse. So faith is defined as "that which comprehends as fact what cannot be experienced by the physical senses." Another way of saying this is that faith perceives as real fact what has not yet been revealed to the senses. This is what Jesus meant when he said that whatever we ask in prayer, believe that we have received it and we will. So faith is taking God at his word. This is easier said than done. But this is the foundation of faith that can move mountains.

Prayer:

Lord, I am so absorbed by what I see and feel. I need your Holy Spirit to lift my vision into your spiritual realm to see the unseen, which is eternal.

Hindrances to Faith

For the weapons of our warfare are not
worldly but have divine power to destroy
strongholds. (2 Corinthians 10:4)

If faith that brings results is not easy, what is the problem? One day, I was praying for divine healing. I asked the Lord to give me a word for direction. I was led to the passage in 2 Corinthians. Paul talks about the reality of spiritual warfare—that we have spiritual weapons and divine power to pull down strongholds.

A spiritual stronghold is when our enemy has a foothold in our lives that hinders us from experiencing his power and receiving what he has promised. I had heard of this teaching on stronghold but thought that it applied to the nonbeliever, certainly not to me as a Christian and minister of many years. So I asked the Lord what he meant and kind of halfheartedly asked if I had a stronghold. I was somewhat surprised when he said yes. "What is it?" I asked. "Your attachment to the world of senses, what you see and what you feel." Wow! I began to understand that the hindrance to my healing was that my physical symptoms were more real than the unseen power of the Spirit.

My faith was based more on what I saw and felt. So when I prayed for healing and only saw and felt my symptoms, there was no faith left. I was looking to see my healing rather than see my healing as a real fact not yet revealed to my senses.

I am not suggesting that our physical senses are not real. I am suggesting that there is a higher reality in the spirit realm. This reality is where our focus should be. This is the realm Jesus reveals. So dear reader, what strongholds may be keeping you from experiencing his power more fully? What has a higher priority in our life, ambition, acceptance, fear, worry, attachment to things, or others? Ask the Lord. He will show you, if you really want to know.

Prayer:

Lord, in what way has the enemy established a foothold in my life that I need to pull down in your name?

Another Perspective

We once regarded Christ from a human
point of view, we regard him thus no
longer. (2 Corinthians 5:16)

I have already indicated how the world of physical
senses can hinder us. It is Paul who reveals to us
the true perspective for the believer. It is so simple
that we missed it. I did for a long time. In this passage, Paul tells us that they once looked at Jesus
from a human point of view, but not any longer. They
saw Christ as who he is—our Lord and Savior. So if
anyone is in Christ, he is a new creation. So just as
we don't see Jesus from the human point of view,
we don't see others or the world or our lives simply
from the human point of view. We see Jesus in all
his glory as the image of the invisible God. "The
one for whom and by whom all things were created"
(Colossians 1:15). And so we don't look at our fel-
low Christians from a human point of view. We see

each other as new creations in him. The old has passed away, and the new has come. We focus on the old rather than the new. So as Christians, we are to cultivate seeing our world and each other from God's perspective. We look for the hand of God in all aspects of our lives. We see holy possibilities where others see none. We see God's goodness where others see none. We set our sights on how God works for good in everything.

In what way do you need to begin to cultivate this perspective?

Prayer:

Lord, I want to see beyond my present circumstances and see you in all of your goodness and power.

Making God Known

No one has ever seen God; the only Son...
he has made him known. (John 1:18)

One of the ways I develop my God perspective is to
begin the day focusing on God the Father. I affirm
who the Father is. He is my life, my source, my
strength, and my health. He delights in giving me
the kingdom. I let my mind dwell on what belongs to
the kingdom (Romans 14:17; 1 Corinthians 4:20)—
joy, peace, healing, righteousness, and power.

I continue to meditate on such truths: He is
the giver of only good things (Matthew 7:11). He is
faithful when we are not (2 Timothy 2:13). He has
given us a spirit of sonship not fear (Romans 8:15).
Therefore, I can cry Daddy, Daddy, Daddy. I have
easy access as His child. I affirm that his grace is
sufficient, that he doesn't treat me the way I deserve
(Psalm 10:10). As I focus on the character of the

father, my heart is filled with gratitude and joy. What a way to begin the day.

Prayer:

Lord Jesus, thank you for revealing who the Father is and who I am in him. I want to walk in the truth and the power of who the Father is.

Jesus the Son

And this is the testimony, that God gave us
eternal life, and this life is in his Son. He
who has the Son has life (1 John 5:11)

Another way I cultivate a divine perspective is to
begin the day focusing on who Jesus is and how he
impacts my life. Not only does he offer me eternal
life; he offers me life here on earth that is abundant.
Life full of good things, health, strength, faith and
purpose. I meditate on such truths as that he chose
me before I chose him. Me, with all of my human
failings. He knows all about me and still chose me.
For what? To be his friend. Jesus is my friend who
accepts me as I am. Who will listen to my deepest
needs, fears, hurts, and disappointments. He lis-
tens, supports and encourages. In all of my circumstances, he is there to love. His life flows through
me. He is my vine. I am his branch. Because of
this he promises that I will be fruitful and that my

fruit will abide. (John 15: 5,15,16). I am healed by his stripes. He has transferred me from the kingdom of darkness and into his kingdom of light. So with a friend like Jesus how can I be discouraged or defeated?

I don't have many friends like that. Do you? He promises that in Him I will be fruitful and that my fruit will abide. (John 15:5,15,16)

His life flows through me. He is my vine. I am his branch. How can I be discouraged or defeated with a friend like that? How can you?

Prayer:

Forgive me for letting my circumstances distract me and keeping me from seeing what a powerful friend you are. Now I see clearly who you are and rejoice in your friendship.

Mind and Spirit

To set the mind on the Spirit is life
and peace. (Romans 8:6)

The Holy Spirit is God's way of working in our lives today. Yet there is much ignorance of the Holy Spirit among Christians today. So another way I cultivate the divine perspective is to focus on what the Bible has made known. The Holy Spirit brooded over the unseen world and brought the creation into manifestation as God spoke the word. He was there at the beginning. The Holy Spirit gives us a new birth that places us in God's family (John 1:12). The Holy Spirit who dwells in us offers to us all of these benefits—he can quicken our bodies with new life, a spirit of sonship, helps us in our weakness, intercedes for us, seals us for our heavenly inheritance, is greater than the devil, can do more than we can think or ask, and is the immeasurable greatness of his power in us who believe. The same Spirit that raised Jesus from the dead dwells in *us* (Romans 8:11)._The Holy Spirit produces lasting fruit in us and bestows supernatural gifts of power and revelation (1 Corinthians 12:7). As I meditate on who the Holy Spirit is and what he offers to me, my heart is filled with wonder and praise. I feel emboldened and ready for whatever the day holds.

Prayer:

Thank you, Lord, for the gift of your Holy Spirit. I choose to walk in confidence and power because the same Spirit that raised you from the dead dwells in me.

Wrong Voices

The devil said to him, "All these I will
give to you, if you will fall down and
worship me." (Matthew 4:8–10)

One evening, during prayer, I was reflecting on my walk with the Lord. I found myself reviewing my shortcomings, my spiritual indifference, my lack of fruitfulness, and my self-absorption. I found myself falling into a negative attitude and a sense of self-condemnation. I became very critical of myself. Have you ever been there? As I was sinking into this spiritual oppression, the Lord spoke to me and said that I was listening to the wrong voices. I was listening to the whispers and accusations of my enemy. I thought that I was just dealing with the old nature. There is some truth to this. However, the real truth is that our enemy uses this to oppress us and rob us of the joy of our salvation. So the Lord threw me a lifeline, teaching me not to listen to the wrong voice but to listen to his. It is what he says who I am that counts.

No matter what my faults and failings are, I am his and a joint heir with Christ. My oppression was lifted, and I learned a valuable principle for my walk with the Lord. Be careful whose voice you are listening to. Jesus learned this when he was tempted.

Prayer:

Deliver me from the wrong voices. Help me to recognize only your voice.

Strengths not Faults

Love is patient and kind. (1 Corinthians 13:7)

My wife and I were visiting a new church that had been started in Germantown, Tennessee. We were intrigued by the name, Cathedral of Praise. I thought it was a community church but discovered that it was an Assembly of God church whose pastor was led to start it through a vision. Everything was first class in this newly constructed church. Before the floors were covered, various scripture verses were written. So it could be said that wherever you were standing, you were standing on the word of God. We found this church to be open to the moving of the Holy Spirit and enjoyed worshiping there. One Sunday morning as we were praising the Lord and seeking his presence, I received one of those small still voice messages that caught me by surprise. The Lord said to me, "You see your faults, but I see your strengths." Wow! Could this be true? As you already know, I sometimes get down on myself because of my faults. I sometimes would wonder why the Lord puts up with me.

Have you ever wondered that? Out of his loving kindness, the Lord was letting me know his perspective of me. I see my faults, but he sees my strengths. Isn't that just like our Lord? This is how the Lord sees you too. Take this to heart and rejoice.

Prayer:

Lord, help us to see ourselves as you see us.

DAY THIRTEEN

Denial of Self

If any man would come after me, let
him deny himself and take up his cross
and follow me. (Matthew 16:24)

Jesus made it clear in this passage that to be serious in following him, there are two conditions. One is denial of self. Second is taking up our cross. I have come to understand these two principles somewhat differently than the traditional view of many. There is a difference between denial of self and self-denial. Self-denial is when we deny ourselves things. During the season of lent, just before the celebration of the resurrection of Christ, we often hear many say, "I'm giving up sweets for lent," or some other item or habit they consider unhelpful. This is self-denial.

Denial of self goes deeper. It is denying ourselves that part of us that hinders us in our walk. This is a long-time denial of self, not temporary.

For example, I deny myself the human right to be offended. Or I deny myself the human right to self-pity or jealousy or resentment, etc. No one had more of a right to be offended or resentful or self-pity than Jesus. But he did not. So as a Christian, I follow his example. This doesn't mean I never have these feelings, but I deny myself the right to indulge in these, but then I give them to the One who can set me free. As a young Christian committed to the ministry, I was profoundly impacted by a pastor who led me to Christ. He had a hearing loss and wore hearing aids. He said to me one day, "Many say to me what a cross you have to bear." Then, he said to me that this or any other handicap is not a cross. It may be a burden or aggravation but not a cross. A cross is voluntary, something you take up in order to follow Jesus. My cross may be losing a job or mistreatment or rejection or persecution because of my faith. So what has following Jesus cost you? What denial of self or voluntary sacrifice have you had to make in order to follow Jesus?

Prayer:

Lord, help me see what part of self I need to deny or what sacrifice I need to make to follow you more fully.

No Denial

If we are faithless, he remains faithful for he cannot deny himself. (2 Timothy 2:13)

Shortly after I retired, I found myself wondering what to do. I kind of felt like I had lost my moorings. I didn't have to be anywhere—no hospital visit, no sermon to prepare, or no meetings to attend. So I began to reflect on my past life in the ministry—reliving highs and lows. I saw the ugliness of my times of rebellion, self-pity, and self-indulgence; and I cried out to the Lord, "Why have you put up with me?" His answer to me was this passage. The words stood out, when we are faithless, he is faithful because he cannot deny himself. Here was the answer.

God put up with me not because of my goodness or good works but because he is my heavenly Father who cannot deny this. In other words, God is stuck with us. I must say that I felt like shouting with joy. The puzzle of God's permanent attitude for us had been settled.

Let this encourage you.

Prayer:

Father, thank you for loving me so and helping me to walk in this confidence.

Just ask

Ask and it will be given you. (Matthew 7:7)

I am what one would call an introspective person. I analyze and evaluate myself. So with my prayer life, I often analyze my prayers. Are they good enough? Is my faith strong enough? Am I praying right or effectively? This is not bad in itself, but it does seem to indicate a high degree of self-absorption, which could be a hindrance to an effective prayer life. One day, when *I* was doing this, I was taken aback by what the Lord said to me. He said, "Stop analyzing your prayers and just pray." Really? Was it that simple? This is what Jesus seemed to be saying in our scripture above. I have found that often, my casual prayers are the most effective, where I just ask and in faith wait for the answer. Perhaps, we make prayer more complicated than necessary. Should I pray standing or sitting? Should I pray in the morning or evening? Should I pray in a certain mood or anytime? Maybe it is that simple. Stop analyzing. Just pray.

Prayer:

Lord, help me to trust you more. Keep my prayers simple and honest.

Christ in Me

Christ in you the hope of glory. (Colossians 1:27)

That Christ is in us defies our rational understanding. We generally understand that this is possible through the Holy Spirit who came to take the place of Christ on earth. Nevertheless, Paul is quite firm in declaring this. Some time ago, I read about an experience of the founder of the Christian and Missionary Alliance Church. This gave me a new insight into the meaning of this truth. A. B. Simpson was the founder of this church group. I don't remember where I read this, but I acknowledge that this is not original with me. The story is that A. B. Simpson would often pray, "Lord, make me more loving, more kind, more faithful, etc." But he always fell short of these qualities. One day, while praying in this way, the Holy Spirit interrupted him by saying that he would always fall short. However, Christ will always be all loving, all kind, all faithful, and never change. A. B. Simpson said that he learned a new way of praying. He no longer prayed to be made this or that. He simply prayed, "Lord Jesus, be you in me." This gave me a whole new direction for my prayer life.

My prayer is:
Lord Jesus, be you in me.
This can be your prayer too.

$\mathcal{F}ear\ \mathcal{N}ot$

Fear not for you will not be ashamed;
you will not be confounded, for you will
not be put to shame. (Isaiah 54:4)

I had decided to take some steps of faith regarding my health. It was not long before I discovered that I was in over my head. I had taken some steps that made me vulnerable to some high risks and possible failure. I was completely dependent on God for my healing. I struggled with my fears, especially fear of failure and shame. I had placed my life in God's hand, and I was determined to trust God. My symptoms got worse, and I would cry out to God for a word of encouragement. God was faithful. On one of these days, I was crying out to God, and he led me to this passage. This was not one with which I was familiar. Although the words were directed to a time of distress for Israel, it spoke to my need. Often, scripture has a dual application—one for the time and period it was written and one for today. This passage read, "Fear not, for you will not be ashamed; be not confounded for you will not be put to shame" (Isaiah 54:4). How loving and caring is our God. I don't know what hard circumstances you are facing or what overwhelming fears you may have. These words from Isaiah may be just what you need. God will not let you down. He upheld me, and He will uphold you.

Prayer:

Thank you, Lord, for caring for me and keeping me in your hand.

Works for Good

We know that in everything God
works for good. (Romans 8:28)

I was sixty-six, and I thought I had made it through without any life-threatening illness. I was asymptomatic, but my cardiologist wanted me to take a heart test. I agreed to show him that there was nothing wrong. He was being overly concerned. Have you ever thought that? The result was that I had five clogged arteries—not two, three, or four, but five. My cardiologist seemed ecstatic when this was discovered, but me, not so much. I was in a state of shock. A surgical nurse came in to give me the news. When he got to five, I cried out, "Stop! That's enough."

As I laid there in the recovery room, it began to dawn on me how serious this was. I began to feel panicky and cried out to the Lord, *Why?*

I had been serving him for many years; I even taught others that he was our healer. So how could this be? I was just a little upset that he allowed this to happen. Do you know what I mean? It was in the midst of these feelings that God spoke to my heart with that soft inner voice I had come to know so well. He said, "Harold." God always called me Harold, not Chris, which is what others called me. "Harold." This does not take me by surprise. "All of my resources are available to you for your healing." A great calm and a deep peace came over me. It was not something I conjured up, not positive think-ing or even self-encouragement.

It was God's presence—God's peace that passes all understanding. From that moment on, I knew that all would be well. Even in this, the Lord was working for good. I came though without any setbacks or complications. That year, I had three more surgeries, including one for prostate cancer. And in my later years, I also had three more sur-geries, including a heart valve replacement. After the valve replacement, my cardiologist here told me that he didn't think that I was going to make it. My heartbeat was thirty-five. A heartbeat of sixty-five was normal. Through all of this, I would hear the words, "Harold." This doesn't take me by surprise. "All of my resources are available to you for your healing." So dear reader, whatever life-threatening circumstances you are facing, God is not surprised; and all of his resources are available to you for healing. Praise God!

Prayer:

Thank you, Lord, that you know all about me and my circumstances and are there to demonstrate your power and loving care.

Blameless

Even as he chose us in him before the
foundation of the world, that we should be holy
and blameless before him. (Ephesians 1:4)

As I have indicated in previous meditations, I have
struggled with trying to be good enough or doing
enough to justify my salvation. I have also indicated
how I discovered that God's grace was sufficient. So
you can understand how pleased I was to learn that
it had always been God's plan to make us accept-
able to him. In these verses, Paul declares that it
was God's intention from before the creation to pre-
destine us in Christ to be presented to him holy and
blameless. Wow! Could this be true? I didn't have
to get stressed out trying to earn my salvation. It
was God's gift in Christ. He would see to it that we
would appear before Him not by anything we did,
but by everything he did in Christ. Can you imagine
my relief? No matter my imperfections or sin-prone-

ness, I would be presented to God holy and blameless. When I look at myself, this seems far out of my reach, but not God's. This is reinforced by John 3:2 and Romans 8:29. So will you give up any idea that you can earn or deserve your salvation by anything you can do and rejoice in the security that is yours as a believer in Christ? Can you shout *praise the Lord*?

Prayer:

Thank you, Lord, for the confidence we have that one day we will reflect your image and glory.

Heaven and Earth One

As a plan for the fullness of time, to unite
all things in him, things in heaven and
things on earth. (Ephesians 1:10)

Many of us have wondered about God's will. What
is God's will? Is it good or evil? The answer usually
is that we can know God's will and that it is good
because Christ reveals it in his deeds and teach-
ings. Yet there is still a mystery about God's will. So
many bad things are blamed on God's will that we
get confused. The same is true about God's will for
the future. I have read these verses in Ephesians 1
and have found great comfort. But for some reason,
this particular verse got my attention. The mystery
about the future has been revealed. The day is coming when heaven and earth will be one. This defies
our rational understanding. But it seems quite clear.

Heaven and earth will be united in Christ, and
we who are believers will be a part of this heaven

on earth kingdom. Let your imagination run with this truth. What we have learned about life on earth can be used in heaven. The spiritual principles we have learned here can be used there.

Some things on earth are overwhelming. Nothing in heaven will be overwhelming except possibly God's love and living presence. Be encouraged by this and press on. Live your life now in light of the future that is yours in Christ.

Prayer:

Lord, how wonderful is the life you have prepared for us. We give to you all of our fears, worry, and anxiety. They mean nothing compared to the glory to be revealed to us.

Fallen Christians

You are severed from Christ... you who have
fallen away from grace. (Galatians 5:2–4)

Paul can be called the apostle of Grace. So it is
understandable that I was stunned when I read
these verses. I have never heard a message or
teaching on these verses. It kind of was like a slap
in the face. Paul is asking the Christians at Galatia
why they were giving up their freedom in Christ and
taking on the yoke of slavery—slavery to the law
of circumcision. This requires salvation by what
we do. Watchman Nee in his book *The Normal
Christian Life* has made a startling statement about
grace. He wrote that if we experience any degree
of self-condemnation, it is because we are not
depending on God's grace. This really spoke to me
for this is what I was doing. I was prone to self-condemnation because of my sin. Paul uses stronger
language that we need to hear. If we are trying to

justify our salvation by anything we do, we have fallen away from grace. Take heart, this is not a condemnation but an assurance that God's grace is all that we need. So rejoice in the freedom that is yours in Christ.

Prayer:

Forgive us Lord that we act like what you did for us on the cross needs some supplemental work by us.

Signs for Believers

And these signs will accompany those who believe... they will lay their hands on the sick, and they will recover. (Mark 16:17)

I mentioned my experience with the Holy Spirit in the "Introduction." Soon after that, I witnessed my first dramatic healing. A neighboring pastor had requested that I visit a member of his church who was a semi-invalid. I did not know what the condition was, but it was serious enough to cause her to be bedfast. As I was driving to her home, I became anxious. I thought to myself, *This is serious.* I wasn't sure my faith was up to this. I was considering going back home and waiting until I felt stronger spiritually. Just then, I heard a still small voice. It was the Holy Spirit speaking to my spirit. The Spirit said, "You are not going in your name. You are going in the name of the Lord Jesus Christ." So I continued on. I arrived at a small one-room house. When I knocked, I was invited in. I saw a middle-aged woman in bed with a painful expression on her face. Her unemployed husband sat near her looking quite dejected. I wasn't sure what to say. I introduced myself and told her that I had come at the request of her pastor. Then, I asked her if she believed that God could heal her. She replied that she had read a book on healing.

Then, I felt an inner boldness come over me. I laid my hands on her and said, "In the name of the Lord Jesus Christ, rise and walk." I couldn't believe that those words came out of my mouth. She got out of bed, stood there, and cried. I thought to myself, *It didn't work*. So I asked her what was wrong.

She cried out, "It's gone. It's all gone." She was pain-free. I told her to keep praising the Lord and left. A couple of weeks later, I read in the local paper a letter from a reader describing her bedfast condition. The initials of the person writing were the same as the lady I had prayed for. I thought she had a relapse. It took me a few days before I had the courage to revisit her.

She was still healed and had written that letter before her healing. Don't you love how God puts up with our doubts and unbelief? I have learned not to underestimate what God can do in spite of us. Take heart, dear reader, because God loves you just as you are and wants to demonstrate his healing power through all who believe, even if it is a little shaky. Isn't this his promise in Mark 16? Are you a believer? Then, rejoice, because you are a candidate for miracles.

Prayer:

Lord, your promises are amazing. Help us to trust you to keep your promises. What step of faith would you like for me to take?

Spiritual Gifts

Earnestly desire the spiritual
gifts. (1 Corinthians 14:1)

Since my baptism with the Holy Spirit mentioned in the "Introduction," I began to see other gifts of the Spirit such as prophesy and a word of knowledge and wisdom. My first experience with prophesy happened while attending a worship service in an Assembly of God Church. During the time of worship and praise, God gave me a prophecy. It had two parts. I thought there were two prophecies, but turned out to be one. Both parts were for the same person. One part of the prophecy was that there was a person there who had a deep long-standing hurt that had robbed that person of their joy. This person was to give this to the Lord and forgive the hurt. If so, there would be fullness of joy. The other part was that this person also had a long-standing physical pain. If this person would place their hand on their chest, they would be healed. I got out of there as soon as I could. I didn't want to find out how wrong I was. A few days later, I received a letter from a lady who had attended the service at the suggestion of a friend. The prophecy was for her. She forgave the hurt and was filled with joy. She also had the pain and placed her hand on her chest, and the pain left. I was humbled and amazed at the new power at work in me. This power is for all believers who are ready to receive.

Prayer:

Lord, I want all that you have for me, whatever the cost.

DAY TWENTY-FOUR

Word of Knowledge

To one is given through the Spirit the utterance
of wisdom, and to another the utterance
of knowledge. (1 Corinthians 12:8)

Little did I know that God was going to show me
more of his power. There were other gifts than prophecy. I was to discover God's power in the word of
knowledge and wisdom. There may be other ways
these gifts are experienced. However, this is how I
experienced them. The traditional definition is that
a word of knowledge reveals facts about a person
or situation not known by natural means. A word
of wisdom reveals instructions for how to respond
to the word of knowledge. My experience has confirmed this. I was holding an evangelistic meeting in
a large church in northern California.

As I was preparing the Sunday evening service, the Lord made known to me through a word
of knowledge that there would be a young man in

the service whom he had called into the ministry. However, family and friends discouraged him, and he was ready to give up on this call. I was to tell this young man that the call was of God and that if he was obedient, God would bless him richly.

During the evening service, a young marine sang a solo. As he sang, the Lord told me that this was the young man that He had told me about. The young marine left the stage and began to walk out. Since I was not yet in charge of the service, I couldn't stop him. So I prayed that the Lord would stop him.

Suddenly, a man stopped the marine and began to engage in a conversation.

The service was turned over to me by the pastor, and I called the marine to come forward. He did. I told him what the Lord had revealed to me, and he confirmed that it was true. He felt called to the ministry, but his family and friends had ridiculed him, and he decided to get a degree in music instead of theology. But he declared that now, in light of what the Lord made known to me, he would answer the call of God on his life. Praise God!

I was amazed at how much God loves us. He loves us so much that he would use a frail human being in such a personal way. He is a God of details.

Again, I want to encourage you to be open to all that God wants to do in and through you. Learn more about this wonderful power of the Holy Spirit and the gifts of the Spirit. This is for all believers.

Prayer:

Lord, I don't understand all of this. I do need and want more power in my life to be and to do that you want me to do. Fill me with your Spirit.

Kingdom Power

For the kingdom of God does not consist in
talk but in power. (1 Corinthians 4:20)

This passage had always bothered me because
I saw such a lack of power in our individual lives
and the life of the church. Paul is talking about the
supernatural power of the Holy Spirit as exhibited in
the New Testament Church. For me, supernatural
power was spooky and conjured up all kinds of wild
things. Having experienced that power, I now see
that the supernatural is natural to God. Who needs
a God who only works naturally? So now, I want to
share with you another experience with the gifts of
the Spirit—the word of knowledge (facts not known
by natural means) and word of wisdom.

Note that this is a word not knowledge or wisdom in general, just a word. God uses these gifts
and more to meet needs and demonstrate his divine
power. I was teaching a course in a local Bible col-

lege. On the way to the class at a stoplight, it was revealed to me that there would be a student in the class in need of healing. Much prayer had been offered for healing, but none came. I was told that the student had become discouraged and thought healing was not God's will. I was to tell that student it was God's will and pray for her healing. As I began my lecture, the Spirit reminded me of my mission. I stopped and informed the class what had happened and asked who the student was.

A young woman stood up and said it was her. She continued, "I prayed that if healing was God's will that he should reveal it to you, brother Christmann."

Wow! God does care for us and will use us for his glory. I almost missed it.

The whole class prayed, and she was healed. This is not an isolated demonstration of God's power at work in us. This is the fulfillment of the promise of Jesus (John 14:12). This power is available to all believers if you are willing to receive it (Luke 11:13).

Prayer:
Lord, fill me with your Holy Spirit.

Pleasing Faith

And without faith it is impossible to
please Him. (Hebrews 11:6)

I have discussed the difference between intellectual
faith and faith that takes risk. When I first started to
prophesy, I was afraid of making a mistake.

When it comes to the working of the Spirit, we
do fear making a mistake.

I prayed, "Lord, how can I know it is really
you through your Spirit and not just me?" I was a
preacher and could repeat scripture and give exhor-
tations. So I asked the Lord to give me a safe way
of knowing it is his Spirit at work in me.

I was not prepared for his answer. He said that
I could never be 100% sure. Since his Spirit had to
work through an earthen vessel, there would always
be the risk of making a mistake. That is why a step
of faith is required. We walk by faith, not sight. This
wasn't very helpful, but I have learned that as I

step out by faith, I have become more confident. But there is always the risk of making a mistake. In almost all of the healings of Christ, a step of faith is required. I assure you my brother and sister—it is worth the risk to see the power of God at work in us. My challenge to you is: What step of faith is the Lord asking of you?

Prayer:

Lord, I want to see more of your power at work in me. Show me what step of faith you want me to take.

God's Reward

For whoever would draw near to God must believe that he exists and that he rewards those who seek him. (Hebrews 11:6)

I volunteered for a recall to active duty as a navy chaplain to serve in Vietnam. My motives were a combination of patriotism and a desire to escape some uncomfortable personal circumstances. I had avoided the activation of my reserve unit to Korea because I had declared myself for the ministry. So now, I had the opportunity to serve in combat. So I volunteered to go to Vietnam. I was unhappy with some personal things.

So I used this opportunity to run away from them. I'm not proud of this.

But God used all of this to his glory. I'll share how, later. When I arrived in DaNang, Vietnam, late at night, I fell into a spiritual and emotional dark place.

What have I done? I thought. I was overcome with homesickness. So I prayed, "Lord, if I go by my feelings, I would find a dark corner and hide for the duration of my tour. Lord, if you can use me in this state of mind, I am willing for you too." God was faithful and enabled me to see many conversions to Christ, answers to prayer, and healings. One of the most unusual instances of God's grace and sense of humor was a young marine and his pet monkey.

Twelve hour days, seven days a week, was normal. One evening after a long day, I had just gone to sleep. There was a knock at my door, and a young marine came in saying, "Chaplain. Chaplain, I need to talk with you. It is urgent. The commanding officer has ordered that everyone get rid of all pet monkeys. I can't do this. I love this monkey more than anything, and he loves me more than anyone." I was a little irritated. I was not in the monkey business. However, I sensed that inner prompting that made me realize that God had something in mind. I heard that still small voice that said, "Tell him about my love." So I asked the marine that if I told him about a love that would never give up on him, never fail him, and would always be there for him, would he be interested. He quickly replied, "Oh yes, Chaplain. I need that kind of love." So I told him about Jesus and that he should kneel at the altar and ask Jesus to come into his heart. He did this and became quite excited. He was experiencing the risen Christ. He began to praise God in a new language and was filled with the Spirit. As I was rejoicing in what the Lord was doing, the marine stopped and shouted out, "Chaplain, I am going to get my monkey. He needs this kind of righteousness too." I thought, *God, what a sense of humor you have.* I told the marine that it was not necessary to get his monkey but that he should return to his quarters thanking the Lord for what he was doing.

Prayer:

Lord, help me to be sensitive to your leading and use me to touch someone's life today by your love.

Power Not Talk

But you shall receive power then the Holy
Spirit has come upon you. (Acts 1:8)

I was sent to Japan and assigned to a Marine
Aircraft Group (MAG). The group would be moving
into Vietnam, and I was to help prepare them for
this.

I became acquainted with a young missionary and his family. We became close friends. One
Saturday morning, I was engrossed in sermon
preparation.

Ministers don't like to be bothered at such times.
This didn't seem to bother God. I began to sense
that inner prompting I have mentioned before. I
shrugged it off. Imagine I was too busy for God.
When I finished my preparation, the prompting per-
sisted. After some resistance, I went to visit my missionary friend, only to discover that he was deathly
sick.

He was supposed to meet a pastor friend at the nearby airport, but was too sick to do it. I laid my hands on him and prayed as once before, "In the name of Jesus Christ, rise and walk." He cautiously got out of bed and stood up. After a few moments, he said that he felt good and left to meet his pastor friend. He told me later that he had to drive through a smelly fishing town on the way and thought, *If I make it through this village without getting sick, I will know that I am healed.* Dear reader, do you think that God looks down on us and smiles at our frail faith?

Prayer:

Lord, help me to talk less and walk in your divine power.

Manifest Presence

He who loves me will be loved by my
father, and I will love him and manifest
myself to him. (John 14:21)

As I indicated in the "Introduction," I was listening
to a video by Evangelist John Bevere. He made a
statement that really challenged me. He said that
everything God had done for us in Christ was so
that we could have intimacy with him. As I pondered
this, I began to see that—yes, the cross, forgiveness, salvation, the gift of the Spirit, and eternal life
had one thing in common. Now, we can have intimacy with God. We may not want it. But it is available. Then, the evangelist made another statement
that opened up another level of understanding. He
said that we talk about God's presence and how
God is with us always. "This is true," he said. "But
what we need is God's manifest presence."

This filled a need I had of long-standing. I longed for God's presence but thought that it was not realistic. After all, we had the assurance that the Lord was with us always. And that is a great comfort. But now I know there is something more to experience of God's presence—his manifest presence. Jesus promised this. The experiences I have shared with you are evidence of God's manifest presence. There is much more for the believer to experience. It is there. Did Jesus not promise if we seek, we shall find; if we ask, it will be given to us; if we knock, it will be opened to us? In the Greek, these verses can be translated as seek and keep on seeking, ask and keep on asking, knock and keep on knocking. So dear believer, don't be satisfied with less—seek more of God.

Prayer:

I am a needy person. Lord, manifest your presence according to your promise.

Divine Fellowship

Our fellowship is with the Father and with
his Son Jesus Christ. (1 John 1:3)

When I was a prison chaplain, I met with all of the
new inmates. I would ask two questions: (I) How
many believed in God? (2) What difference did that
faith make in the way they lived their lives? All said
that they believed in God. None said that it had
made any difference. This may describe many of
those who say that they believe in God. The word
"believe" means to live by.

So when I say, "I believe," it is more than intellectual—it is experiential.

So I ask you: How experiential is your faith?
This is not meant to lay a guilt trip on you. Any suc-
cessful athlete realizes that there is always room
for development, more to achieve. He sets high
goals. In my own spiritual walk, I have been lazy,
taking the easy way out, coasting on what I know.

The challenge for us believers is to press on—don't stay stuck; don't be satisfied with just getting by. We are called to be more than conquerors. How are we doing? How are you doing? God has so much more for us than we have experienced.

Determine that you will seek and find it. Where are you stuck spiritually?

What holds you back? What fears or doubts hold you captive?

Prayer:

Lord, whatever is holding me back, whatever fears or doubts have a grip on me, set me free. I am an overcomer through my faith in you.

Freedom from Fear

There is no fear in love, but perfect
love casts out fear. (1 John 4:18)

I have been retired for many years. Life was good.
I was active, secured financially, and enjoying
God's blessings. Without any warning or symptoms, I began to have anxiety attacks. There were
no apparent reasons or circumstances that war-
ranted such attacks. They could come at any time,
but were especially strong just before waking up. I
would find myself fighting waking up for fear something bad was going to happen. This went on for
six months or more. I was distressed and weak-
ened in strength. The psychological term for this
was "free-floating fear." This was not helpful, since
there were no circumstances justifying such fears.
I would pray, but nothing seemed to help. Then
one late evening, God spoke to my heart as I was
sleeping. He said to me, "Harold, you don't need

to be afraid to wake up. Because when you do, you will wake up to my love and grace, the same love and grace that have brought you through so much." Wow! I thought, *That is right. God's love and grace have brought me through a lot.* I don't know why I didn't think of this or affirm this before. This is exactly what God states in 1 John 4:18—again, the wonder of God's intimate love. How wonderful to experience a moment of God's intimacy when he just speaks the word to you that you need. If you haven't yet experienced this, don't give up. Listen for that small still voice and you will. If you have had such a moment, rejoice for there are more to come. God wants intimacy with us.

Prayer:

Thank you, Lord, for caring about me in all of my circumstance. Forgive me when I am slow to turn to you in my moments of anxiety and fear.

Thank you for hearing me when I do.

Appendix

1. I mentioned in my meditation for "Day Twenty-three" that in 1960, there was a supernatural move of the Holy Spirit that resulted in many Christians across denominational lines receiving what was called the baptism with the Holy Spirit. Many signs and wonders with the gifts of the Holy Spirit were manifested.

   Since this may not be known by many of my readers, I refer you to a book by an Episcopal priest named Dennis Bennett and the impact this had on his church and others. The book is *Nine O'clock in the Morning* (Bridge Logos).

2. Another book that may be of interest to my readers is one by Pastor Jack Hayford on the baptism with the Holy Spirit and what it means for us today (Chosen 2004).

3. For those desiring more information on the gifts of the Spirit, I recommend the book "The Gifts of the Holy Spirit" by Derek Prince (Whitaker House 2007).

4. Many people find God's will to be a mystery, especially since God is blamed for many tragedies that happen today. As a young minister, I found a book by Leslie Weatherhead, *The Will of God* (Abingdon Press1999), to be very helpful in understanding the ways God exercises his will today.

5. Clinical pastoral education involves special training for ministers in a clinical approach to ministry. It involves intensive psychological training and personal interaction and analysis similar to clinical psychology.

All scripture verses used are from the Revised Standard Version, Second Edition. World Bible Publishers, 1972.

Reader Reviews

1. Reading *Moments of Divine Intimacy* has helped me to realize how alive the gospel is and how much more the Holy Spirit wants to work in my daily life.

   Alan Evarts, CEO, Evarts Interiors Inc., servicing Ventura County, California, for forty years

2. Ch. Christmann's *Moments of Divine Intimacy* has stirred up a desire in me to let the Holy Spirit in me do more. The truths Ch. Christmann have shared has helped me to relax and to depend upon God more. It has helped me to draw near to the Lord and be open to my own moments of "divine intimacy."

   Margaret Willey, housewife and mother

3. It has been said that experience is the best teacher, but it does not have to be your own. We can learn from others. In his book, *Moments of Divine Intimacy*, Ch. Christmann has revealed

some spiritual nuggets of truth. I recommend this book for the believer in Jesus Christ who is desiring a deep walk with the Lord. Brother Christmann proves the saying, "a man with an argument is no match for a man with an experience."

Rev. Delvin Hurt, retired Assembly of God minister

4. Ch. Chris as his friends call him is one of my favorite mentors. He is also one of the most humble men I know. I am inspired by his honest reflections, both in personal discussions and in his book of devotions, *Moments of Divine Intimacy*. It is a pleasure and privilege to recommend it.

Jan Clark, businesswoman

5. I am impressed with the simplicity of presentation of God's grace and the personal way in which God wants to manifest his power in us. I highly recommend this book, *Moments of Divine Intimacy*, to all who seek to draw near to the Father and desire to see his power at work in their lives.

Dr. Edward O. Irobi, contributing faculty, College of Health and Sciences, Walden University

6. After reading *Moments of Divine Intimacy*, I was impressed by the message of faith and acting on God's leading. In James 5:17, there is a reference to one of the most powerful figures in the Bible, the prophet Elijah. James writes that Elijah was a human being as we were. Elijah prayed earnestly that it would not rain. And it did not rain for three and a half years. The emphasis in this verse is twofold—first, that Elijah was a human being, and second, that God answered his prayer. Elijah walked with God and was intimate with him. A person filled with the Spirit of God is able to interact with God and see things happen. According to 1 Corinthians 12:11, the Spirit of God distributes gifts as he wills. It is up to us to use the gifts the Spirit makes available and to develop them to the glory of God. The practical application of these principles is demonstrated in Ch. Christmann's devotional. I found it inspiring and encouraging to continue exercising my faith and my walk with God.

Dwight Spilman, production control administrator in the space industry.

CPSIA information can be obtained
at www.ICGtesting.com
Printed in the USA
FSHW02n0605130618
49124FS

9 781641 403986